ANN ROSSI

Moving North

AFRICAN AMERICANS AND THE GREAT MIGRATION

1915—1930

NATIONAL GEOGRAPHIC

Washington, D.C.

PICTURE CREDITS

Cover (clockwise) Florida State Archives, Phillips Collection, Washington, D.C.; **pages 2-3** © CORBIS; **pages 4, 6-7, 9** (top), **10, 12** (bottom), **17, 22** Library of Congress; **pages 5, 16** (bottom), **32** © 2004 Gwendolyn Knight Lawrence/Artists Rights Society (ARS), New York; **pages 9** (bottom), **23, 24, 31, 36** Brown Brothers, Sterling, PA; **pages 11, 12** (inset) **14, 30, 35** © Bettmann/CORBIS; **page 13** Chicago Defender, Chicago, IL; **page 15** Archive Photos, NY; **pages 16** (top) **26, 27, 33** (top), **34** The Granger Collection, NY; **page 19** Florida State Archives; **pages 20-21** Henry Hammond/Archive Photos, NY; **pages 25, 28** National Archives; **page 29** Schomburg Center for Research in Black Culture, NY; **33** (bottom) © Underwood & Underwood/CORBIS; **page 38** Museum of the City of New York/Archive Photos, NY; **back cover** (top to bottom) The Granger Collection, NY (2); Archive Photos, NY; Hulton Getty/Liaison Agency; Library of Congress

QUOTATIONS

Page 5 From COLLECTED POEMS by Langston Hughes, Copyright © 1994 by the Estate of Langston Hughes. Reprinted by permission of Alfred A Knopf, a Division of Random House, Inc. **Page 9** William Crosse, "The Land of Hope" in the Chicago *Defender* **Page 10** From *12 Million Black Voices* by Richard Wright (NY: Thunder's Mouth Press, 1988), p. 67 **Page 13** From *Journal of Negro History*, July and October, 1919, quoted in *The Black Americans* by Milton Meltzer (NY: Thomas Y. Crowell, 1984), p. 169 **Page 14** From an article written by Dr. W. E. B. Du Bois in *The Crisis*, a journal, in 1919, quoted in *The Black Americans*, p. 188 **Page 19** From *12 Million Black Voices*, p. 99 **Page 20** Text quote: From *American Hunger* written in 1944 by Richard Wright, as quoted in *Up South*, edited by Malaika Adero (NY: The New Press, 1993), p. 116; From *12 Million Black Voices*, pp. 99-100 **Page 21** From the Chicago *Defender* in March 1917, as quoted in *Up South*, edited by Malaika Adero (NY: The New Press, 1993), pp. 210-211 **Page 22** From *The Big Sea* by Langston Hughes, (Hill and Wang, 1940), as quoted in *The Black Americans*, p. 166 **Page 28** From "The Exodus Train" from *They Seek a City* by Arna Bontemps and Jack Conroy (NY: Doubleday, a division of Bantam Doubleday Dell Pub., Inc. 1945), as reprinted in *Up South*, pp. 214-215 **Page 31** Excerpt from "Harlem Reconsidered" originally appearing in *Freedomways*, Fall, 1964, by Loften Mitchell, as quoted in *The Black Americans*, p. 207 **Page 32** By James Weldon Johnson, as quoted in *Bound for the Promised Land* by Michael L. Cooper (NY: Lodestar Books/Dutton, © 1995), p. 61

Library of Congress Cataloging-in-Publication Data

Halpern, Monica.
  Moving north : African Americans and the Great Migration, 1915–1930 / by Monica Halpern.
     v. cm. — (Crossroads America)
  Includes index.
     trade ISBN: 0-7922-8278-7
     library ISBN: 0-7922-8358-9
  Contents: Slaves no more : life in the South, 1865-1915 —Opportunities in the North — We are leaving! — A new life — The Harlem Renaissance — The Depression hits. 1. African Americans—History—1877–1964—Juvenile literature. 2. African Americans—Migrations—History—20th century—Juvenile literature. [1. African Americans—Migrations. 2. African Americans—History—1877–1964. 3. Migration, Internal. 4. African Americans—Social conditions.] I. Title. II. Series.
E185.6.H2145 2006
304.8'089'96073—dc22

                                  2003019833

Produced through the worldwide resources of the National Geographic Society, John M. Fahey, Jr., President and Chief Executive Officer; Gilbert M. Grosvenor, Chairman of the Board; Nina D. Hoffman, Executive Vice President and President, Books and School Publishing.

PREPARED BY NATIONAL GEOGRAPHIC SCHOOL PUBLISHING

Ericka Markman, President, Children's Books & Educational Publishing Group; Steve Mico, Senior Vice President & Editorial Director; Nancy Laties Feresten, Vice President & Editor-in-Chief, Children's Books; Marianne Hiland, Editorial Manager; Anita Schwartz, Project Editor; Tara Peterson, Sam England, Editorial Assistants; Jim Hiscott, Design Manager; Linda McKnight, Art Director; Diana Bourdrez, Anne Whittle, Photo Research; Matt Wascavage, Manager of Publishing Services; Sean Philpotts, Production Coordinator; Jane Ponton, Production Artist; Susan Kehnemui Donnelly, Children's Books Project Editor. Production; Clifton M. Brown III, Manufacturing and Quality Control.

PROGRAM DEVELOPMENT
Gare Thompson Associates, Inc.
CONSULTANT/REVIEWER
Dr. Russell L. Adams, Professor and Chair, Afro-American Studies, Howard University
MAPS Equator Graphics

Copyright © 2006 National Geographic Society. All rights reserved. Previously published as *The Great Migration* (National Geographic Reading Expeditions), copyright © 2002.

NATIONAL GEOGRAPHIC SOCIETY
1145 17th Street, N.W.
Washington, D.C. 20036-4688

Printed in Mexico

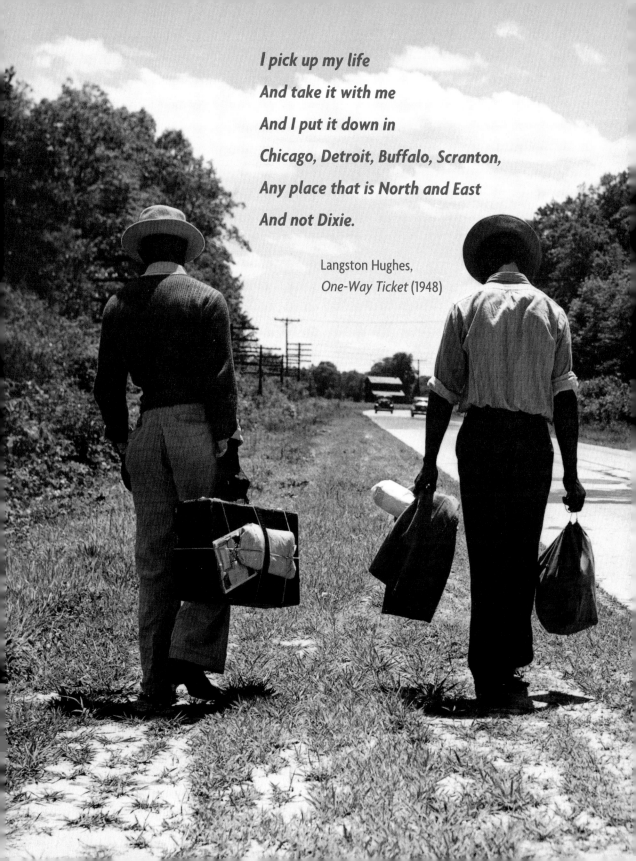

I pick up my life
And take it with me
And I put it down in
Chicago, Detroit, Buffalo, Scranton,
Any place that is North and East
And not Dixie.

Langston Hughes,
One-Way Ticket (1948)

Leaving the SOUTH

Why would someone want to leave everything that was familiar and move to a distant place? Many African Americans did. They wanted to leave the South. From 1915 to 1930 thousands and thousands of African Americans **migrated**, or moved, from the South to the North. This movement is called "The Great Migration."

Life in the South was still very difficult for many African Americans after the Civil War ended in 1865. The Thirteenth Amendment had abolished slavery, but for many, freedom was only the first step on the long path toward a better life. Most African Americans in the South still worked as farmers, and few owned their own land. They were very poor and lived in small, run-down cabins. Their children had little chance for an education.

African Americans wanted to be able to earn a good living, to own property, and to move ahead. They wanted a safer and better life for themselves and for their families. Many believed that moving to the North would make their hopes and dreams come true.

COLORED
WAITING ROOM
PRIVATE PROPERTY
NO PARKING
Driving through or Turning Around

Chapter 1

SLAVES No More

Life in the South, 1865–1915

The Civil War ended slavery but left the South a ruined land. The nation's lawmakers wanted to rebuild the South in a new and better way. The rebuilding of the South was called **Reconstruction** (1865–1877). In 1865 Congress set up the Freedmen's Bureau to help make life better for the freed African Americans. The Bureau provided food, clothing, housing, medical care, jobs, and schools. Congress passed laws giving African Americans the right to vote, hold office, and own land. At last, African Americans would have equal rights.

Many people in the South were not ready to accept African Americans as equals. They wanted things to remain as they had been before the Civil War. Southern states passed laws called Black Codes. These laws limited African Americans' right to own land and to work and live where they wanted. Some codes set curfews and allowed officials to arrest unemployed African Americans.

As southern lawmakers regained power, they continued to make it hard for African Americans to improve their lives. By 1877 Reconstruction was over. African Americans had lost many of the rights they had gained.

Voting Restrictions

After Reconstruction ended, southern lawmakers passed laws to keep African Americans from voting. Some states required voters to be able to read and understand any section of the state constitution. Without an education, most African Americans could not do this. Other states required voters to pay a **poll tax** which kept the very poor from voting. Still other states required voters to own a certain amount of property. Few African Americans owned property. Without the right to vote, African Americans could not choose their leaders.

Jim Crow Laws

Southern lawmakers passed other new laws that limited the rights of African Americans. These **"Jim Crow" laws** required the **segregation,** or separation, of white and black people. Blacks and whites could not be educated at the same schools or treated in the same hospitals. Blacks had to sit in separate sections in restaurants, movie theaters, public parks, and on public transportation.

Earning a Living

As slaves, most African Americans had been trained to make a living by farming. Without an education, few could do anything else. Once the Civil War ended, most African Americans stayed near or on the land they had worked as slaves. Most became **sharecroppers,** renting and working land owned by white landowners.

Each spring, sharecroppers borrowed money to buy seed and fertilizer. After the harvest, the sharecroppers had to pay back what they owed. They split their earnings with the landowner and kept whatever was left. In some years, the farmers did not make enough money to pay back all they had borrowed. They sank ever deeper into debt.

Education

Every family member was needed to work on the farm at busy times of the year, even the youngest. Most African American children had little time to go to school. Yet African Americans wanted their children to have an education. Education was their only chance to make a better life for themselves.

The separate schools for African Americans were poor in every way. School buildings were old and poorly equipped. The few textbooks were old and out-of-date. Classes were large. Teachers were poorly trained, if at all. And the school year was so short that students could receive only the most basic education. However, African Americans found strength in their own community.

A school for African
American children

Community Life

African Americans created their own communities. Living far out in the country, they could not use town services. Their land was often poor for farming. Their houses were small, usually just one or two rooms. But families and neighbors helped one another through difficult times. They depended on each other. In time their communities grew.

The center of the African American community in the South was the church. Here most social events took place. Families gathered on their one day of rest, dressed in their best. Many traveled long distances to visit with friends and family.

Ministers were often community leaders, better educated than most. Many were excellent speakers. Going to church was a time to celebrate and to share. African Americans relied on their churches to give them comfort and hope.

Voices from America

"Sunday is always a glad day. We call our children to us and comb the hair of the boys and plait the hair of the girls;...In clean clothes ironed stiff with starch made from flour, we hitch up the mule to the wagon, pile in our Bibles and baskets of food—hog meat and greens—and we are off to church."

Chapter 2

Opportunities in the NORTH

Even though life in the South was difficult, many African Americans found ways to lead satisfying lives. After all, the South was home. One problem, however, could not be avoided. That was the threat of violence.

African Americans had to follow strict rules of behavior, such as having to step off the sidewalk to let a white person pass by. If they broke a rule, they might be insulted, attacked, or even killed. To find safety for themselves and their families, many African Americans began to think about moving to the North.

War Brings Opportunity

World War I (1914–1918) brought new opportunities for African Americans. Northern factories were booming with orders for war materials. There were few workers. Many men were fighting in the war. Workers from Europe could not come to America because of the war. So, where could factory owners find workers?

African Americans found jobs working in the Hudson River Tunnel connecting New York and New Jersey.

Factory owners looked to African Americans in the South as a new source of workers. They sent labor **recruiters** south to find and hire workers to move north. The recruiters offered jobs in the factories and steel mills, in meatpacking houses, and on the railroads.

The recruiters made many promises about the wonderful life African Americans could have in the North. Some offered decent, well-paying jobs and the possibility of good housing, fine schools, and safety. They sometimes offered free or cheap train tickets. The recruiters brought hope of a better future, a chance for African Americans to fulfill their dreams.

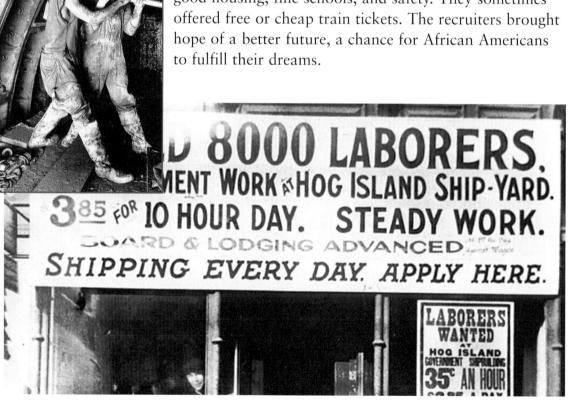

D 8000 LABORERS. ᴹᴱNT WORK ᴬᵀ HOG ISLAND SHIP-YARD. 3 85 FOR 10 HOUR DAY. STEADY WORK. ᴮOARD & LODGING ADVANCED. SHIPPING EVERY DAY. APPLY HERE. LABORERS WANTED AT HOG ISLAND GOVERNMENT SHIPBUILDING 35¢ AN HOUR

The News Spreads

Black-owned newspapers spread the news about job opportunities in the North. These newspapers were widely read. The Chicago *Defender* became black America's most popular newspaper. Articles in the *Defender* urged African Americans in the South to move north. The newspaper reminded them of the many problems they faced in the South.

As more and more African Americans decided to move north, they looked to the newspaper for help. They wrote hundreds of letters to the *Defender* asking for information about jobs, housing, education, and transportation. Here is a letter from a poor farmer in Anniston, Alabama. He wants an education for his children, something he was not able to get in the South.

April 23, 1917

Dear Sir:

Please gave me some infamation about coming north I can do any kind of work from a truck gardin to farming I would like to leave here and I cant make no money to leave I ust make enough to live one please let me here from you at once I want to get where I can put my children in school.

MEET *Robert Abbott*

Robert Abbott was an African American who started the Chicago *Defender,* a weekly, in 1905 after migrating north from Georgia. His newspaper's readership grew rapidly. By the late 1920s, Abbott claimed that he was sending out 250,000 copies of the paper weekly. He used railroad workers to leave copies of the *Defender* all over the South. Readers passed their copies on to others until the newspapers were worn out. Abbott used his newspaper to encourage African Americans to seek a better life in the North.

Letters Home

News of opportunities in the North continued to spread. Many African Americans in the South had relatives and friends who had already left for the North. Letters and visits from them painted a rosy picture of life there.

Returning Soldiers

More than 300,000 African American soldiers were sent to Europe during World War I. In France, these soldiers were treated well. Returning home, soldiers could no longer put up with being treated poorly in the South. Many left for the North.

Voices from America

"This is the country to which we Soldiers of Democracy return...
    We return.
    We return from fighting.
    We return fighting.
    Make way for Democracy!
We saved it in France, and...we will save it in the United States of America or know the reason why."

Against Migration

As African Americans left the South by the thousands, many southern whites became alarmed. The South's **economy** depended on the labor of African Americans. Farm and household workers were almost all African Americans. Cotton farming, in particular, needed many workers at certain times of the year. If African Americans left, who would do this work?

Some southern whites suggested improving wages and protecting African American lives and property. Others used force to stop African Americans from moving north. Laws were passed to stop recruiters from talking to them. Often people handing out the Chicago *Defender* were beaten or jailed. Police sometimes arrested African Americans who were trying to board trains going north. In one small southern town, the railway station was closed. People in the town thought that would stop African Americans from moving north.

15

The South Is Our Home

White Southerners were not the only people who objected to the migration of so many African Americans. Some African Americans feared they too would lose their livelihood if too many black people left the South. Some church leaders tried to prevent members of their congregations from moving north. Many small business owners wanted their customers to stay in the South. Some African Americans were deeply attached to the land that had long been their home.

Booker T. Washington ▼

Booker T. Washington, an important African American leader, opposed the migration. He said: "[I have] never seen any part of the world where it seemed to me the masses of the Negro people would be better off than right here in these southern states."

For thousands of African Americans, however, nothing could stop them from moving to cities in the North. The glowing reports and constant encouragement from friends, relatives, the press, and labor recruiters were too powerful.

▲ **Jacob Lawrence, The Great Migration Series #3**
African Americans leave by the hundreds to go north.

Chapter 3

We Are LEAVING!

Migrants chose a destination, or place to go, in the North based on where they lived. Since they usually had little money, they chose the cheapest and most direct route. African Americans who lived along the Atlantic **coast** usually traveled directly north to the coastal cities of Philadelphia, New York, and Boston. Those who lived in Mississippi, Arkansas, and Louisiana usually went to Chicago, Detroit, and Milwaukee.

The departure of thousands of African Americans changed the landscape of the South. The arrival of African Americans in the cities of the North changed things there, too.

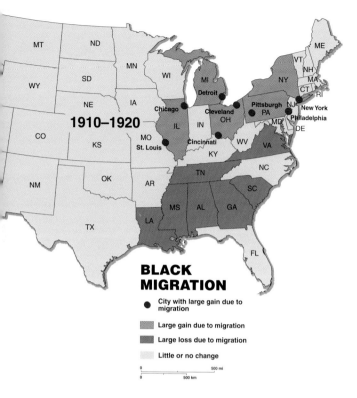

1910–1920

BLACK MIGRATION

● City with large gain due to migration

Large gain due to migration

Large loss due to migration

Little or no change

0   500 mi
0   500 km

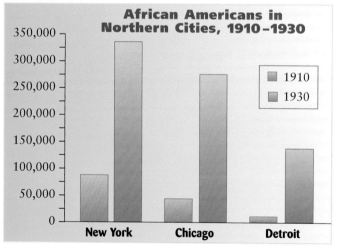

African Americans in Northern Cities, 1910–1930

■ 1910
■ 1930

▲ The African American population more than tripled in three northern cities as a result of the Great Migration.

The Migration Grows

It took great courage for African Americans to leave their homes, families, friends, jobs, and communities. Few of the migrants had ever traveled more than a few miles from home. Moving north was a huge and scary step.

Single men were the first to move to the North. They left their families behind. They could earn more money in the North. Their plan was to send money home until they were settled. Then they would bring their families north. Single women came next. They found plenty of opportunities for work, mainly as household workers but also in factories.

As good news trickled home from earlier migrants, the stream of migrants grew to a river. Soon, entire families came. Whole neighborhoods and church congregations moved together. Finally, doctors, clergymen, professionals, and business people followed their clients and customers north.

We're On Our Way

For many, the first step on the trip was to get on a train going north. Poverty kept some from making the trip. The train fare from New Orleans to Chicago was about $20, a month's pay for most workers. Still, people found a way. Railroads offered special fares for groups traveling together. Railroad workers and their families could travel for free. Labor recruiters gave out free passes. Travel by ship from port city to port city was a little cheaper than the train. Some migrants worked their way north.

Migrants wrote slogans on the sides of the trains expressing their feelings. "Farewell—We're Good and Gone," and "Bound for the Land of Hope" said it all.

Richard Wright, a very successful and well-known African American writer, moved north from Mississippi as a young man. He wrote about his train trip:

> We look around the train and we
> do not see the old familiar signs:
>
> **FOR COLORED** *and* **FOR WHITES**

Reaching the Promised Land

The train trip was the first sign that life in the North really would be better. But once off the train, the migrants found "towering buildings of steel and stone." For the first time, they heard strange sounds. "Streetcars screeched past over steel tracks. Cars honked their horns." What a shock after living on the quiet green farmland of the South!

The migrants had reached their new home, but now they had many problems to solve. They needed places to live, jobs, and schools for their children. They wanted a church to worship in and a welcoming community to give them comfort. Organizations were formed to help the new migrants make the move from **rural** to **urban** life.

One such organization was the National Urban League. Formed in 1911, the organization began job-training programs to prepare new migrants for factory work. They also helped migrants find jobs and housing. They gave out clothing and held classes in good housekeeping and good citizenship. The Urban League was one of many organizations that African Americans set up to help one another.

Fitting In

Thousands of largely uneducated southern blacks were pouring into northern black communities. People who had come north in earlier migrations were well established by now. Because there had been so few early migrants, they had not upset local white society. They had jobs and some financial security, and their children went to decent schools. The earlier migrants feared that the uneducated and country ways of the new arrivals would increase race **prejudice** and **discrimination** against African Americans.

To help the new migrants be accepted, the Chicago *Defender* continued in its role as adviser by describing how to behave in northern cities:

> *Be clean...water is cheap....Avoid loud talking, and boisterous laughter on streetcars and in public places; ...In the South they don't care how they dress; here they make it a practice to look as well in the week as they do on Sunday.*

SELF-HELP

1. Do not loaf. Get a job at once.
2. Do not live in crowded rooms. Others can be obtained.
3. Do not carry on loud conversations in streetcars and public places.
4. Do not keep your children out of school.
5. Do not send for your family until you get a job.
6. Do not think you can hold your job unless you are industrious, sober, efficient, and prompt.

Cleanliness and fresh air are necessary for good health. In case of sickness send immediately for a good physician. Become an active member in some church as soon as you reach the city.

The Chicago Urban League provided these tips to help African Americans from the South adjust to life in the North.

Voices from America

"I went out walking alone to see what the city looked like. I wandered too far outside the Negro district,...and was set upon and beaten by a group of white boys....I came home with both eyes blacked and a swollen jaw. That was the summer before the Chicago riots."

▲ The National Association for the Advancement of Colored People (NAACP) flew this flag outside its New York City offices each time an African American was lynched.

Violence Again!

The early black migrants were not the only people who objected to the newcomers. Many northern white people were **hostile** to them as well. Some Northerners were frightened by the Southerners' different ways. Workers feared the competition from so many new job seekers. They were afraid that their jobs might be taken by the new arrivals. In some cities, white-owned newspapers added to the poisonous atmosphere with such headlines as:

ARRIVE BY THE THOUSANDS— PERIL TO HEALTH

Sometimes whites dealt with their fears and anger through violence. Riots erupted in many cities. The summer of 1919, called the Red Summer, was especially bad. There were about 25 race riots. The worst one was in Chicago.

African Americans had hoped to escape violence by leaving the South. The riots had destroyed those hopes. In the future they would try to make their own community stronger and safer by sticking together.

Chapter 4

A New Life

Thousands of migrants had arrived in every major city in the North. Filled with hope, they began a new life. In many ways, their lives did improve. Most migrants found jobs and these jobs paid much better than any in the South. African American children were expected to attend school. Northern schools were generally better than southern schools. African Americans could vote for their leaders. African American business people and professionals had more chances to build successful careers.

Life in the North was certainly not perfect. Finding work and a place to live was not easy in the big city. For many southern migrants, it was their first time in a city.

Voices from America

"[A] landlord could take a six-room apartment renting for $50 a month and divide it into six kitchenettes renting at...$192 a month! For each one-room household he provided an ice-box, a bed, and a gas hot-plate. A bathroom that once served a single family now served six."

Housing

Most migrants arrived in the big, strange cities without family and friends. Life in the cities was very different from life at home. They wanted to be near people they knew or who were from the same area in the South. Having the people, churches, organizations, and foods of the South nearby made them feel comfortable.

The migrants were not allowed to live in many areas because of segregation. They also had little money. So most migrants moved to districts where only African Americans lived. Popular areas were Harlem in New York, the Hill in Pittsburgh, the South Side in Chicago, and Paradise Valley in Detroit.

Migrants poured into these rapidly growing neighborhoods. Some of the housing was comfortable and roomy. Many families took in lodgers, often friends and relatives from the South. These lodgers helped pay the rent.

However, much of the housing in African American sections was in need of repair. As more and more migrants arrived, there were not enough houses for them to live in. Housing became overcrowded, and rents became expensive.

Factory Work

Once the migrants had found a place to live, they had to find work. One of the major reasons southern blacks moved north was for job opportunities. In the South most migrants had worked in farming or as household workers. In the North many migrants found work in factories. These jobs were in steel mills, automobile plants, stockyards, meatpacking plants, and clothing factories.

Working indoors in factories was a big change from farming. Factory workers had to work 10 to 12 hours a day, 6 days a week. Adjusting to a new way of working was not easy. But migrants were grateful for better-paying work. They earned more money than they ever had before. A week's wages in a factory might be as much as $25. This was a high salary for a farmworker earning 75 cents a day.

African American women found jobs in clothing factories. They were paid for each item they finished, not by the hour.

The Middle Class

Not every migrant found work in factories. Many business people and professionals followed the thousands of migrants north. Drugstores, restaurants, funeral homes, moving companies, and other businesses found plenty of opportunities within African American communities.

Most African Americans who succeeded in the business world provided essential services to their communities. One of the wealthiest women in New York was Mary Harris. She made her fortune selling pigs feet on the streets of Harlem out of a baby carriage!

MEET Madam C. J. Walker

Madam C. J. Walker was one of many successful African Americans in the business world. She developed her own business selling hair and skin preparations to the black community. She began her business with only $1.50 and a recipe for a hair-care product. By 1915 she had more than 2,000 people selling her products, and she was a millionaire.

Business people and community leaders urged all African Americans to make their dollar do "double-duty" by buying from blacks. They would then be buying what they needed and also "advancing the race."

Some African Americans opened their own businesses, such as banks and insurance companies. One such business, the Liberty Life Insurance Company founded in 1919, became one of the nation's largest African American-owned insurance companies. It won African American support through advertisements such as this one.

At last! At last! The Negroes are going to get together.... If we ever expect to get anywhere as a race of people we must first learn to stick together.

Community Life

City life was not just about work. African Americans joined or formed organizations, such as social and political clubs. Voting was very important to them. In some elections they voted in larger numbers than white voters. The migrants had not been able to vote in the South.

As they grew in numbers, the African American communities also grew in political power. No politician could ignore them any longer. In some places laws were passed protecting the rights of African Americans. These laws forbade landlords, schools, and other public places from keeping African Americans out.

The Press

The African American press played an important role in educating and informing the African American community. Like the Chicago *Defender*, new African American newspapers carried news and information that other newspapers ignored. All black newspapers had two roles in their community: to report the news and to encourage African Americans to stick together. One newspaper, the Chicago *Whip*, sponsored the "Spend Your Money Where You Can Work Campaign."

The Chicago *Defender* remained the most widely known African American newspaper. It cost a dime a copy. Thousands bought and read it or read it to others. Nearly everyone in Chicago's South Side discussed it.

MEET the National Negro Baseball League

African Americans were not allowed to play America's most successful professional sport, baseball. A few African American baseball clubs played informally. In 1920 Rube Foster, one of baseball's great pitchers, established the National Negro Baseball League. Through the 1920s, eight teams in this league played before loyal fans. Most of the teams had their own parks. Sometimes they played exhibition games with white major league teams. Baseball players earned salaries of about $2,000 a year.

The Church

Probably the most important institution in the African American community was the church. The church had been the center of the community for most African Americans living in the South. In their new home migrants looked for a church where they felt comfortable. Northern established churches held formal services demanding "proper" behavior. Uncomfortable there, many newcomers started their own churches in people's homes or in storefronts.

Church leaders helped migrants find jobs and housing. Churches offered social clubs, child care, summer camps, classes, and homes for the aged and for orphans. Most importantly, African American churches provided a friendly place for migrants to escape the problems of everyday life. Many members spent most of their free time in religious activities. Some churches held nightly services.

Chapter 5

The Harlem Renaissance

By the 1920s the African American communities in many northern cities were exciting, lively places. The mix of southern and northern black cultures created a new black culture. The center of this new cultural life was Harlem. Harlem was a prosperous section in northern New York City.

Harlem became the center for a **renaissance,** or rebirth, of the arts. Many talented musicians, artists, actors, poets, and writers were drawn there. African American literary and political magazines appeared. Well-known political and cultural leaders gave lectures. The library on 135th Street became Harlem's cultural center. Harlem was an exciting place to be.

Harlem

At the turn of the century, Harlem was home to new immigrants from many countries. Poles, Germans, Irish, and Italians lived in the neighborhood with African Americans. Trees shaded the wide avenues. Fine **brownstones** and modern apartment buildings lined the streets.

In the early 1900s, large numbers of migrants from the South began to move into Harlem. Harlem was the nicest neighborhood in which African Americans could live.

Soon, many white people who lived there began to leave in large numbers. They sold their property cheaply. They were sure that real estate prices would drop because so many African Americans were moving into their neighborhood.

Real estate companies bought these properties. They then sold or rented them at high rates to the African Americans eager to move into Harlem. Harlem became an African American neighborhood.

Rent Parties

For people without much money, paying rent was often hard to do. To help pay the rent, people held rent parties in their apartments. The host provided food, music, and a place for dancing. The guests paid an admission fee, perhaps 25¢. These parties were also a good way for newcomers to meet each other.

The Good Life

By 1920 Harlem covered less than two square miles and had a population of about 80,000. Although it was crowded and expensive, people were eager to live there. Harlem was jumping with life. The area was well-known for its many restaurants, theaters, and clubs.

On Sundays everyone in Harlem relaxed. Dressed in their best, some people strolled up the main street, Seventh Avenue. Others sat on the front steps of their buildings. They wanted to experience the rich and exciting sights and sounds of Harlem.

The Harlem Renaissance

In the 1920s writers, artists, and musicians gathered in Harlem. These artists called themselves the New Negroes. They shared a spirit of pride, self-respect, and independence. They believed their art would help African Americans win a more equal place in American society.

The Harlem Renaissance included all the arts. But its writers were perhaps the best known. Poems, stories, and plays by African American writers were published by magazines for both black and white audiences. In 1925 one of these magazines, *Opportunity*, held a literary contest to encourage new black writers. The winners included Zora Neale Hurston and Langston Hughes. The work of these two writers is still read and enjoyed today.

▲ Jacob Lawrence, Migration Series #53

Zora Neale Hurston

Zora Neale Hurston was one of the few women in the Harlem Renaissance. Called "a genius of the South," she wrote seven books and over one hundred short stories, plays, essays, and articles. Perhaps her most popular book today is *Their Eyes Were Watching God.*

Zora Hurston grew up in a small African American town in Florida, one of eight children. Taught by her schoolteacher mother, Zora could read before school age. She read everything she could find, especially novels and poetry.

Many of the stories Hurston wrote were based on her childhood in Florida. They told about ordinary people doing everyday kinds of things. Hurston's books never made much money, but she led an independent life in a time when few women worked outside the home.

Langston Hughes

Langston Hughes wrote novels, stories, plays, and songs. In later years, he also wrote television scripts and hundreds of columns and articles for newspapers and magazines. He was perhaps the best known Harlem Renaissance writer.

Langston Hughes became a poet when he was 14 years old. His eighth-grade class was electing officers. The last officer to be chosen was the class poet. No one in the class had ever written a poem. But the mostly white students believed the **stereotype** that African Americans had natural rhythm in music and poetry. So they elected Langston Hughes class poet. Honored, Langston went home and wrote his first poem. The poem praised his classmates and his teachers. When he read his poem at graduation, everyone cheered! Langston had found his calling in life.

▲ **Edward Kennedy "Duke" Ellington and his orchestra**

The Jazz Age

The writers of the Harlem Renaissance often included the special sounds of Harlem in their poems and stories. The sound they heard most often was **jazz**, the most popular music of the 1910s and 1920s. In fact, the 1920s was often called "the jazz age." Lively and upbeat, jazz symbolized the 1920s.

Jazz was a form of music that was based on African American work songs, spirituals, and the blues. It had its roots in New Orleans starting in the 1890s and early 1900s. New Orleans was a city with people from many different backgrounds and a long musical tradition.

In jazz history Edward Kennedy "Duke" Ellington was one of America's most famous musicians. He was a pianist, a composer, and a bandleader. He wrote over 1,500 compositions and toured the world with his big band.

Chapter 6

The Depression Hits

In the 1920s most Americans had jobs and money. These years were known as the "good times." But then the good times came to an end.

In the South, farmers' crops failed because of drought and boll weevils, insects that destroy cotton plants. African American farm workers lost their jobs. Some industries in the North also began to suffer from bad times. Factories closed and many African American workers lost their jobs.

People became afraid. Many banks failed. People lost their savings. Some people no longer had money to buy goods. With fewer customers, more stores and companies had to close. More workers lost their jobs. By 1931 about one out of three black workers was out of work. The **Great Depression** had hit America.

Please Help Us

Most African Americans had been able to save little money to help themselves in times of emergency. With low salaries and high expenses, they used every penny for their daily needs. Once they lost their jobs, many African American families and individuals were soon in danger of starving.

During the early years of the Depression, only the cities provided public **relief,** help for people during hard times. Only about one in four people without jobs could get relief. In New York City, families were given $2.39 a week to live on. In Detroit, each person received 15 cents a day until the money ran out.

People used their relief money to buy food. They had no money left to pay rent. They were then often **evicted,** or thrown out of their apartments. If they had no family or friends to stay with, they lived on the streets. Communities made up of shacks grew up along railroad tracks or in vacant lots.

African American churches and institutions such as the Urban League did their best to help those in need. Churches offered food, clothing, and fuel. The League helped people find housing, fought evictions, and loaned money.

The Harlem Renaissance Ends

With so many out of work, no one had the money to support the arts. Magazines folded, book sales dropped, and clubs closed. Many artists had depended on rich people to support their art. But even the rich had been affected by the Depression. They no longer could support artists.

Many artists left Harlem, seeking jobs wherever they could find them. Some became teachers. Others with less education worked as laborers. Still others found no work at all.

And so the Harlem Renaissance ended with the Depression. But for the first time, African American artists had been recognized by the entire community, blacks and whites alike. Many of these artists' works are still greatly admired today. Their achievements opened the door for future artists.

Women deliver food baskets to the needy in Harlem.

The Legacy of the Great Migration

The migrants left for the North with great expectations. But the Great Migration turned out to be a mixed blessing for most African Americans. They found new opportunities in the North but also faced new problems.

White residents in the North also experienced new challenges as they met greater competition for jobs, housing, and political power. Many whites were forced to reexamine their attitudes about race and equality.

An important change caused by the Great Migration was the African Americans' growing sense of confidence, economic opportunity, and political power. The struggle to build on these changes would grow in the years ahead.

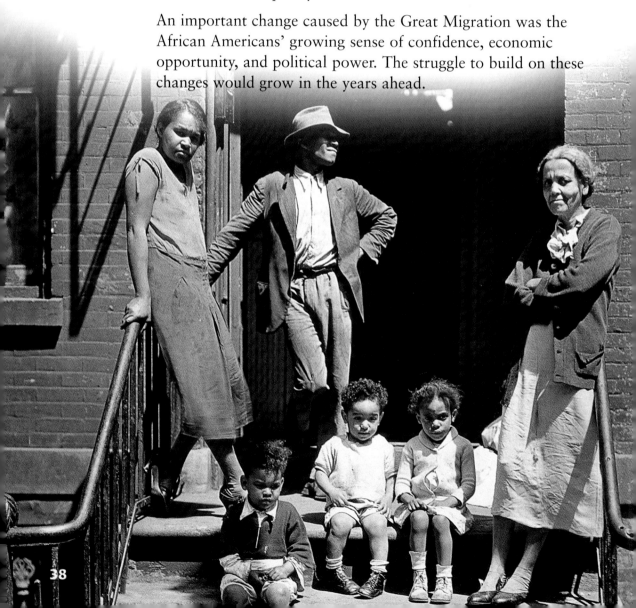